SECRETS
FROM THE PARABLE OF THE
SOWER

WHY SOME MATURE AND MANY DON'T

M.S. Muse

Copyright © 2021 by M.S. Muse

All rights reserved. Except as permitted under U.S. Copyright Act of 1976, no part of this publication may be reproduced, distributed, or transmitted in any form or by any means, or stored in a database or retrieval system, without the prior written permission of the publisher.

Contact information: theparableoftheSower@yahoo.com
Purchase options at: www.theparableoftheSower.com

Print ISBN: 978-0-9884728-2-2
Digital ISBN: 978-0-9884728-7-7

Print Edition: 08/2021
Digital Edition: 08/2021

Unless otherwise indicated, all Scripture quotations are taken from the Holy Bible, New Living Translation, second edition, copyright © 1996, 2004, 2007 by Tyndale House Foundation. Used by permission of Tyndale House Publishers, Inc., Carol Stream, Illinois 60188. All rights reserved.

Scripture quotations marked (ESV) are from The ESV® Bible (The Holy Bible, English Standard Version®), copyright © 2001 by Crossway, a publishing ministry of Good News Publishers. Used by permission. All rights reserved.

Scripture references appear in italics.

Some quotations from church leaders of the past have been modernized for today's readers.

Contents

Introduction		5
Key Passage		7
Chapter 1	The Parable	9
Chapter 2	True Seed	12
Chapter 3	Believe	16
Chapter 4	Good Soil	23
Chapter 5	Three Convictions	28
Chapter 6	Three Deceptions	35
Chapter 7	Fear of the Lord	40
Chapter 8	Humble Repentance	46
Chapter 9	God's Presence	53
Chapter 10	Convinced	62
Chapter 11	Deep Roots	69
Chapter 12	Symptoms	76
Chapter 13	Priorities	82
Chapter 14	Lasting Fruit	89
Chapter 15	Falling Away	99
Chapter 16	Cut Off	104
Chapter 17	Conclusion	109
Endnotes		115

Introduction

My wife and I lived in the Middle East and Asia for much of our thirty-year marriage. We have always been involved in evangelism and discipleship. We have watched new Christians from a wide variety of backgrounds develop in their faith. No matter what their cultural or religious heritage is, some grow quickly while others, sadly, fall away. After many years of wondering why their outcomes were so different, we started to notice a pattern that spanned their diverse backgrounds. We learned we could listen to their testimonies and generally know if they were going to mature quickly or stagnate and likely reject faith in Christ.

The parable of the Sower had always been a mystery to me. It's a simple story, yet just how the ingredients—seed and soil—led to maturity was a question I could not answer. The parable started to make sense when comparing the seed and soil to the testimonies of those who matured versus those who didn't. I realized seed and soil were major themes throughout the Bible. They appear from Genesis to Revelation. This book will connect these themes in hopes that you will mature by the power of the Holy Spirit through the grace of God.

Follow the Parable

Our daughter studied journalism. She wrote articles in college and eventually conducted television interviews in her early career. She shared with me the simple formula journalists should follow. She said, "Make sure you answer the questions what, who, when, where, how, and why." This is a great way to approach God's Word. I've organized this book to answer all of these questions about the parable with an abundance of Scripture. The Bible's teaching on these matters may not be popular today, but every Christian should consider these points carefully.

The "when" and "where" of the parable of the Sower are the past, present, and future here on earth. Those questions are simple. That leaves us with "what," "who," "how," and "why." The seed answers the question "what." The soil answers the question "who." Once we learn *what* and *who* the seed and soil represent, we'll look at *how* God's wonderful gift of salvation takes root in and completely transforms hearts and eternal destinies. In the process, it will become clear *why* many fail to mature and produce fruit.

Now, let's follow the parable and see where it leads.

Jesus Explains the Parable of the Sower

Jesus tells the parable of the Sower to a large group of people. The disciples didn't understand and later ask for an explanation. Jesus relates the meaning.

> *"The seed that fell on the footpath represents those who hear the message about the Kingdom and don't understand it. Then the evil one comes and snatches away the seed that was planted in their hearts. The seed on the rocky soil represents those who hear the message and immediately receive it with joy. But since they don't have deep roots, they don't last long. They fall away as soon as they have problems or are persecuted for believing God's word. The seed that fell among the thorns represents those who hear God's word, but all too quickly the message is crowded out by the worries of this life and the lure of wealth, so no fruit is produced. The seed that fell on good soil represents those who truly hear and understand God's word and produce a harvest of thirty, sixty, or even a hundred times as much as had been planted!"* — Matthew 13:19-23

Chapter 1

The Parable

The parable of the Sower reveals the keys to Christian maturity. In this ordinary story we discover just two ingredients: true seed and rich soil guarantee spiritual growth. Seed and soil represent clear themes woven through the Bible. They promise a miraculous spiritual life when combined in our hearts.

The true seed represents the "*message about the Kingdom*"—that is, the Good News about Christ. Fertile soil is a prepared heart that can *"truly hear and understand"* the message of Jesus. This kind of heart encourages the seed to grow deep roots. These roots allow the shoot to thrive, to endure persecution, and to reject the world's priorities. Deep roots in good soil provide support for the plant to produce abundant fruit.

Spiritual bounty is not the parable's only topic. It also describes soil inadequate for the task. Some hearts may not acknowledge the seed at all. Others seem to accept it in every way; still roots cannot grow deep, plants wither, and genuine fruit never blooms.

Those with unprepared hearts may live their lives adhering to Christian culture, traditions, and expectations. They may affirm the Bible is God's Word. They may even experience the miraculous. Yet, they will fall away, if not in practice, certainly in heart. They won't produce genuine fruit.

Below the Surface

In Luke 18, Jesus tells another story about two men who went to the Temple in Jerusalem to pray. The Pharisee listed his good works as evidence of his spiritual maturity. By all accounts, the tax collector was not spiritually mature. He could only beat his chest in sorrow at a distance, confess his sin, and cry out for mercy. However, Jesus looked at their hearts. He saw what was happening below the surface. Jesus shocked His listeners when He said the tax collector was justified before God, not the Pharisee.

Many concepts of Christian spiritual growth and discipleship focus on behavior we can display, disciplines we can master, and goals we can accomplish. We are taught to be like the Pharisee, to copy what we observe on the surface.

The parable of the Sower is different. Its secrets focus on what is occurring below the surface. It tells us what kind of seed is sown, what kind of soil the seed is planted in, and how roots grow deep. Only when the roots are well established does the plant begin to produce good fruit.

Christian maturity is about what is happening below the surface. Like the parable, we will focus on what occurs in a heart. When that becomes clear, we'll see how these ingredients allow us to thrive spiritually.

So, let's begin with "what." What message do these seeds represent?

Chapter 2

True Seed

What is the true seed in the parable of the Sower?

Secret Plan

The seed in the parable of the Sower represents "*the message about the Kingdom*"—that is, the Gospel, the Good News about Christ. What is God's message? It had been a mystery since the beginning. It remained hidden from humans and angels alike. The Spirit of Christ gave the prophets hints and pictures of a great salvation, but they couldn't imagine what it all meant. They lived their lives longing for something they couldn't grasp or fully describe. Even heaven's angels had to wait. Certain of God's victory, they still had no idea how His salvation would unfold.

> *This salvation was something even the prophets wanted to know more about when they prophesied about this gracious salvation prepared for you. They wondered what time or situation the Spirit of Christ within them was talking about when he told them in advance about Christ's suffering and his*

great glory afterward. They were told that their messages were not for themselves, but for you. And now this Good News has been announced to you by those who preached in the power of the Holy Spirit sent from heaven. It is all so wonderful that even the angels are eagerly watching these things happen. — 1 Peter 1:10-12

Two thousand years ago, Jesus appeared on the earth to accomplish and reveal what generations desperately sought after. The Good News about Jesus is written clearly in the New Testament. His salvation has been preached around the world. This message is the seed of truth. Now we can easily discover the plan angels and prophets waited so long to see!

Mystery Revealed

The New Testament describes God's plan. There are many examples. Below is one from Paul's letter to the Colossians.

This includes you who were once far away from God. You were his enemies, separated from him by your evil thoughts and actions. Yet now he has reconciled you to himself through the death of Christ in his physical body. As a result, he has brought you into his own presence, and you are

> *holy and blameless as you stand before him without a single fault.* — Colossians 1:21-22

Our sin keeps us far away from God. We are His enemies because of our *"evil thoughts and actions."* Yet the death and resurrection of Christ make it possible to be right with our Creator and confidently enter His presence. Jesus makes us pure so we can remain in God's presence for eternity. That's an amazing plan!

Spiritual Message

This message is not something we can easily comprehend. In fact, we cannot understand it without the help of the Holy Spirit. The passage in 1st Peter tells us the Gospel is *"preached in the power of the Holy Spirit."* What is the Spirit saying?

> *"When the Spirit of truth comes, he will guide you into all truth."* — John 16:13a

Just before Jesus suffered and died on the cross, He promised the Holy Spirit would come and reveal the truth. The seed of truth in the parable of the Sower is the same truth the Holy Spirit leads us into, the truth Jesus describes in John 16. He opens our eyes to *"truly hear and understand God's Word"* (Matt. 13:23).

The parable says we can *"hear"* the Gospel and even *"receive it with joy."* That means we can accept it with our minds or our emotions. But that's not enough. The Holy Spirit must open our eyes to the truth.

The disciples remained unaware of who Jesus was in the first part of His ministry. Finally, Peter confessed that Jesus was the Messiah. It suddenly came to him and he blurted it out. Jesus tells him the source of his new understanding.

> *Jesus replied, "You are blessed, Simon son of John, because my Father in heaven has revealed this to you. You did not learn this from any human being."* — Matthew 16:17

The Father had revealed the truth to Peter. We are like Peter. We hear and understand who Jesus is because the Spirit of God shows us.

The Gospel takes firm root in a heart that believes.

Chapter 3

Believe

What does it mean to "believe" the message of the Kingdom?

> *He makes sinners right in his sight when they believe in Jesus.* — Romans 3:26b

When the Holy Spirit reveals the truth of the Gospel message and plants it in a prepared heart, belief is the result. Believing the message of the Kingdom is proof that we hear and understand the truth. Both seed and soil are required to believe. Let's briefly focus on what it means to believe the Good News. Then, in the following chapters, we'll see who readily embraces this message.

> *But these are written so that you may continue to believe that Jesus is the Messiah, the Son of God, and that by believing in him you will have life by the power of his name.* — John 20:31

John explains the purpose of his writing. He wants us to sincerely believe in Jesus and have life. All Scripture has this one goal.

Only Believe

Belief in Jesus is the only requirement for salvation.

> *"We want to perform God's works, too. What should we do?" Jesus told them, "This is the only work God wants from you: Believe in the one he has sent."* — John 6:28b-29

Jesus was speaking to people who were under the Mosaic Law. They pleased God through obedience to this Law and by making animal sacrifices. What a shock it must have been for them to hear Jesus tell them to merely believe in Him. It's even surprising to many of us!

> *"And anyone who believes in God's Son has eternal life. Anyone who doesn't obey the Son will never experience eternal life but remains under God's angry judgment."* — John 3:36

Faith in Christ is the obedience required to enter God's eternal presence. Christ obeyed from His conception through His death and resurrection. We benefit from that very obedience when we put our trust in Him. We are clothed with the purity of Christ the moment we believe. We become His children.

> *Everyone who believes that Jesus is the Christ has become a child of God.* — 1 John 5:1

Belief in Christ is obedience (1 Pet. 1:22). Unbelief is disobedience. The sin of the world is simply unbelief in the Gospel message. By rejecting the truth, God's plan of salvation, one relies on one's own ability to appease God. Those efforts fail. In his first letter, John says those who don't believe the Gospel are calling God a liar! (1 John 5:10). That is a serious charge, but we are all born into unbelief.

> *"The world's sin is that it refuses to believe in me."*
> — John 16:9

What Does "Believe" Mean?

You might assume you know what it means to believe in Jesus. However, many people will be surprised on Judgment Day. They thought they believed but, in fact, they didn't. Let's make sure you know what it means.

This word—"believe"—confused me for many years. My struggle grew when I wondered if I truly believed. How could I claim to be a Christian if I didn't really know what it meant to believe in Jesus? After studying unbelief, I began to understand.

"On judgment day many will say to me, 'Lord! Lord! We prophesied in your name and cast out demons in your name and performed many miracles in your name.' But I will reply, 'I never knew you. Get away from me, you who break God's laws.'" — Matthew 7:22-23

On Judgment Day, unbelievers will experience the Almighty's final rejection. They may have heard and received the Gospel with joy, but they never understood it. Their hearts were not prepared to receive the truth. The seed fell in bad soil.

The *"many"* in verse 22 spent their lives doing Christian works, even supernatural works. I'm sure they went to church and studied their Bibles. But they show their unbelief by the answer they give Jesus. They affirm they rely on their own ability to please God, not on Jesus.

Notice they start their sentence with "We." This proves they believed their own good works would impress God. Their words betray them and confirm their faith is in themselves or their traditions. They believed their efforts or piety could satisfy God's wrath.

Many will say they agree with Scripture. They'll say, "Yes, you have to believe in Jesus to be saved, *but* you also have to . . ." It's more likely they are trusting in what comes after the "but" than in Christ.

The world teaches us our own goodness is very meaningful. This minimizes God's holiness and justice. Do you trust in your above-average moral values, better beliefs, spiritual experiences, or knowledge of the Bible? If you believe these or values like them impress God, then you have faith in your own goodness. Since Christ alone can match God's holiness, faith in Him is the only way to please our Creator (Heb. 11:6). Christian traditions and behavior may seem helpful, but they can't save you from God's wrath. They do not have the power to elevate you to God's standard of holiness.

> *They will act religious, but they will reject the power that could make them godly. Stay away from people like that!* — 2 Timothy 3:5

When you think about how to satisfy God, who do you think of? Do you immediately consider some goodness of your own, or do you humbly praise Jesus for the work He has done for you?

What Is Your Final Answer?

At judgment, our answer must begin with the name of Jesus. "Jesus is the only one who can make me pure in God's sight!" He is the one who has the power to allow us to enter the High and Lofty One's holy, terrifying presence.

> To have faith in Christ means to cease trying to win God's favor by one's own character.
> — J. Gresham Machen

Belief is a continual and confident understanding that Christ is our sole hope of coming near to God today and in eternity. Who is the source of this confidence? It is Jesus who *"initiates and perfects our faith"* (Heb. 12:2). Augustine of Hippo tells us what this faith is: "The only thing I will be able to present to God when I meet Him is my wretchedness and Christ's righteousness."

Belief Leads to Godliness

A godly life is not a requirement for salvation; it is a benefit of believing the Gospel. Belief in Christ allows God's transforming work of grace to begin. In other words, godliness does not lead to salvation. It is salvation that leads to godliness.

How do we manage living in this corrupted world? How do we cope with our fallen nature and the hardships that surround us? We will address the question "how" in later chapters, but John's first epistle gives us a simple and clear answer:

> *For every child of God defeats this evil world, and we achieve this victory through our faith. And*

> *who can win this battle against the world? Only those who believe that Jesus is the Son of God.*
> — 1 John 5:4-5

What Must I Do to Be Saved?

A jailer encounters Paul and Silas in Acts 16. He wants to know what he must do to be saved. As their response shows, it's not a matter of what he must "do." They don't give him a list of rules to follow or works he must perform. It is the message he believes that saves Him.

> *"Sirs, what must I do to be saved?" They replied, "Believe in the Lord Jesus and you will be saved, along with everyone in your household."*
> — Acts 16:30b-31

The true seed in the parable of the Sower is the message that Jesus freely saves all who believe, all who trust in Him for eternal salvation. Now, the parable tells us this message will only root well in a particular type of soil, those whose hearts are prepared.

Chapter 4

Good Soil

Who are those who hear and understand the Gospel?

> *"The seed that fell on good soil represents those who truly hear and understand God's word."*
> — Matthew 13:23a

The true seed in the parable of the Sower points us to the Gospel. It tells us what God's plan of salvation is. All receive the same seed, but in only one kind of soil does it thrive.

The most puzzling aspect of the parable of the Sower is who "good soil" represents.

Missing Ingredient

Good soil is missing in society. Worldly reasoning represents the seed that fell on the footpath, or at least those who have heard and rejected the Gospel. The message doesn't have a chance to root, since it is immediately rejected.

Good soil is missing in many churches. Seeds that land among the rocks and thorns are like those who get involved in church or the Christian religion. They may receive the seed with joy, but they lack the fertile soil required to grow strong. Roots and stems develop, but eventually wither away or remain fruitless.

Many have tried to identify what is missing. They depend on certain types of church services, special teachings or worship styles, better doctrines, or higher moral values to promote maturity. They search above the surface of the heart. However, maturity springs from what is below the surface. In order to identify fertile soil, it will help us to see why the seed by itself is not enough.

The Seed Alone Cannot Save

I invited an atheist to a Bible study. For a year and a half, he heard the Gospel each week. He made many Christian friends and got involved in church. He became more concerned about his moral standards. Finally, he confessed he believed the Gospel. He believed in God. He believed that Jesus was God's son who was sent to save us. There was just one thing he couldn't accept. He didn't believe he had done anything to deserve God's wrath. The Holy Spirit had not convinced him of his sin.

I appreciated his honesty. He knew there was something missing and asked how he could get a sense of his sin before God. It isn't an awareness we can muster on our own. We sat together and prayed. We asked the Holy Spirit to show him his need.

Whom Did Jesus Come to Save?

Jesus tells us exactly whom He came to save: *"For I have come to call not those who think they are righteous, but those who know they are sinners"* (Matt. 9:13b).

Those who have prepared hearts know they are sinners. They understand why they need saving. The Gospel has no spiritual impact without this understanding.

We've spent decades sharing the Gospel with people from many religious and cultural backgrounds. The work of the Spirit easily transcends all of these differences. Eventually we learned that when we hear someone express genuine concern for sin's eternal consequence, we can be sure they'll embrace the truth and grow.

God's freedom is only available to those who are convinced by the Spirit they deserve His wrath. The message of the Kingdom grows in hearts who hear and understand their desperate need for God's mercy.

A Prepared Heart

In chapter 2, we read that Jesus promised the Holy Spirit would come and reveal the truth of the Gospel (John 16:13). We learn from the Spirit what the true seed is. That's not the only work of the Holy Spirit.

Just as there are two key elements in the parable of the Sower, there are two works of the Holy Spirit in John 16. Jesus tells us the Spirit will not only lead us to the truth but also convict us. Seed and soil represent these two works. The Spirit of God leads us to the message of the Kingdom and convinces us of our sin to prepare our hearts.

> *"And when he comes, he will convict the world of its sin, and of God's righteousness, and of the coming judgment."* — John 16:8

The Spirit opens our eyes to a spiritual reality the natural eye can never see. He shows us our sin and compares it to God's holiness. When we realize how far we are separated from God, the consequence of that distance becomes clear. We deserve judgment, and without Christ we will certainly inherit God's eternal wrath.

Sin and Death

> *"That is why I said that you will die in your sins; for unless you believe that I AM who I claim to be, you will die in your sins."* — John 8:24

To die in our sins means we remain far from God for eternity (Rom. 6:23). It means we will experience God's ultimate wrath. Jesus's words may seem harsh, yet they are essential to faith and spiritual growth. The truth becomes much more attractive once we get a clear picture of the great danger we are in because of our wretchedness. The seed of truth grows quickly in a heart the Holy Spirit prepares in this way. It sprouts and thrives! A heart shaped by the conviction of the Spirit trusts fully in the Savior. Conviction makes belief possible.

Remember, the parable of the Sower tells us we can *"hear"* the Gospel and even *"receive it with joy."* This truth can inspire our minds and stir our emotions for a lifetime. We can talk about God and sing His praises. We can be models for others in our church and community. We can even experience the supernatural. But, until the Holy Spirit convinces us we will die in our sins, we are powerless to mature and produce eternal fruit.

Let's take a closer look at the Holy Spirit's work.

Chapter 5

Three Convictions

I often wondered why the work of the Holy Spirit described in John 16 is so specific regarding His conviction: of our sin, God's righteousness, and the coming judgment. These elements seemed so negative to me. They weren't a boost to my self-esteem. However, each of these three revelations is essential to understanding the Gospel. As we'll see, together they give us a clear picture of Christ's work and produce greater love for Him. These three convictions drive us to seek the truth and lead to genuine Christian maturity.

God's Righteousness

> The most damming and evil lie that has ever entered the mind of man was the idea that somehow he could make himself good enough to deserve to live with an all-holy God.
> — Martin Luther

The human mind's concept of God and of our separation from Him is far too limited. It invents a god based on the serpent's temptation in Genesis 3. This god is unreliable, made in our image, and unjust. Without the work of the Spirit, our minds will always yield to the spirit of this world.

The Holy Spirit must give us eyes to see He is the High and Exalted One. He is the Creator of a universe that cannot be measured. His creation is filled with planets, stars, and galaxies that can never be counted. As we consider these distances and God's unfathomable greatness, we begin to see how incredibly small and insignificant we are.

This physical difference between us and God is already impossible to imagine. Yet our spiritual distance from God is even greater. Angels' mighty voices shake the foundations of God's throne room declaring His holiness. The Lord's holiness is emphasized in heaven above all of His other attributes.

> *Attending him were mighty seraphim, each having six wings. With two wings they covered their faces, with two they covered their feet, and with two they flew. They were calling out to each other, "Holy, holy, holy is the Lord of Heaven's Armies! The whole earth is filled with his glory!" Their voices shook the Temple to its foundations, and the entire building was filled with smoke.*
> — Isaiah 6:3

Our Sin

In the ultimate contrast, we inherited Adam and Eve's disobedience. We are not holy. Each of us has willfully sinned against God, just as Adam and Eve did. Our sin is hideous in light of God's incredible purity. This evil exists in our hearts from the moment we are conceived.

> *For I was born a sinner—yes, from the moment my mother conceived me.* — Psalm 51:5

Humans pass an incurable virus from generation to generation (Rom. 5:12). Sin and death are part of our DNA. We are slaves to sin and there is no human cure (John 8:34). We are not willing to fear the Lord, so our sins pile up in God's sight day by day, each one confirming we deserve His wrath.

> *"No one is righteous—not even one. . . . All have turned away; all have become useless. . . . No one does good, not a single one." . . . "They have no fear of God at all."* — Romans 3:10b, 12, 18

Coming Judgment

Jesus tells us He came to save, but to save from what? That critical aspect of the Gospel seems to get lost as the spirit of this world asserts its influence on the Church.

Our rebellion against our mighty Creator makes us objects of His unspeakable wrath. On Judgment Day for those who have faith in themselves, *"they will be punished with eternal destruction, forever separated from the Lord and from his glorious power"* (2 Thess. 1:9). On that day, all will be fully convinced of their own wretchedness (Rev. 6:15-17).

God's judgment isn't temporary, as this life is. It is final and eternal. Revelation 20 tells us Hell is a lake of fire. Most of our descriptions of Hell come from Jesus. He describes it in several ways, including a *"fiery furnace, where there will be weeping and gnashing of teeth"* (Matt. 13:42, 50). This is a spiritual reality. It doesn't matter whether you believe it or not. This everlasting fate is contingent on only one condition.

> *"There is no judgment against anyone who believes in him. But anyone who does not believe in him has already been judged for not believing in God's one and only Son. And the judgment is based on this fact: God's light came into the world, but people loved the darkness more than the light, for their actions were evil."* — John 3:18-19

The Hard Truth

Don't ignore the elements of the conviction of the Spirit when considering the Gospel for yourself or when presenting it to others. Without these ingredients, we will not cultivate fertile soil, but encourage a rocky and weedy environment.

The Bible study broke into small groups for discussion. My group had guys representing every major religion. They were surprised when the passage we were studying revealed that all were destined for Hell without Christ. A Hindu asked if even very good people would receive God's eternal judgment. I told them if we could live a thousand lifetimes, improving in every life, we would still never grow even a millimeter closer to God. Our sinful state wouldn't change a bit, and God's holiness wouldn't bend to our corruption. Two never came back. The rest were drawn to the Gospel, and some eventually believed.

I could have tried to be more diplomatic in hopes all would return. Some would encourage me to avoid the subject of God's judgment altogether. However, I'm convinced both good seed and rich soil are required for salvation and genuine Christian maturity to occur. I have no desire to attempt to make disciples of those whose hearts are unprepared. I bring up some aspect of sin's consequence nearly every time I teach. We never seem to have trouble finding those who long to be pure in God's sight. The Spirit draws them to the truth.

Spiritual Conviction

> That we are so completely sinful, is a truth which no one ever truly learned by being only told it.
> — John Newton

The work of the Holy Spirit is, of course, supernatural. Just as we depend on the Spirit to show us the truth, we also depend on the Spirit to convict us and those around us. Our minds cannot process this spiritual wisdom naturally.

> *Since God in his wisdom saw to it that the world would never know him through human wisdom, he has used our foolish preaching to save those who believe.* — 1 Corinthians 1:21

Human wisdom may grasp some aspects of the Gospel truth. But it can never reveal God's holiness or expose our sin and its consequence. We may be able to explain salvation logically. We may long for God's promises. Yet, these are not enough to give us true understanding of why we so desperately need Christ. The spirit of this world keeps us blinded (2 Cor. 4:4).

In John 16:7-15, Jesus describes the primary work of the Spirit, He opens our eyes to the secrets of good seed and rich soil found in the parable of the Sower. He begins to shine light on our true condition and on God's path to salvation.

Are You Spiritual?

> *But people who aren't spiritual can't receive these truths from God's Spirit. It all sounds foolish to them and they can't understand it, for only those who are spiritual can understand what the Spirit means.* — 1 Corinthians 2:14

Does this all sound foolish? Does the idea of eternal judgment offend your human wisdom? Or do you feel your own goodness can satisfy God's holy standard? In both cases, you prove you aren't spiritual.

> *Pilate said, "So you are a king?" Jesus responded, "You say I am a king. Actually, I was born and came into the world to testify to the truth. All who love the truth recognize that what I say is true."*
> — John 18:37

We sincerely love and seek the truth when the Holy Spirit prepares our hearts by His conviction. However, the spirit of this world is completely opposed to this message.

Satan has opposed it from the very beginning.

Chapter 6

Three Deceptions

All those who fail to grow and produce fruit have one thing in common. They remain under the influence of the spirit of this world. They may have a vague intellectual or emotional understanding of the consequence of their sin. They may call Jesus their savior. Yet, blinded to the realities only available by the Holy Spirit, they go forward in deception.

The Spirit of This World

Satan has been at work deceiving from the beginning. In Genesis 3:1-5, he lies to Adam and Eve. The foundation of his lies are just the opposite of what the Holy Spirit convicts of in John 16.

Unrighteous

> *The serpent was the shrewdest of all the wild animals the Lord God had made. One day he asked the woman, "Did God really say you must not eat the fruit from any of the trees in the garden?"*
>
> — Genesis 3:1

The first lie in the Garden of Eden questions God's righteousness: *"Did God really say . . . ?"* It aims to convince us that God is not holy and what we know of Him from the Bible is unreliable. Those who fall away, as we'll see in later chapters, continue to accept this lie. They embrace it and form a god in their own image, one who agrees with their earthly sense of justice.

No Judgment

> *"It's only the fruit from the tree in the middle of the garden that we are not allowed to eat. God said, 'You must not eat it or even touch it; if you do, you will die.'" "You won't die!" the serpent replied to the woman.* — Genesis 3:3b-4

The second lie tells us to deny judgment: *"You won't die!"* When we remain convinced that God didn't mean what He said regarding the consequence of sin, His wrath must be unjust or a meaningless threat. This makes judgment itself sound unreasonable. It allows us to invent our own criteria for goodness, a standard all "nice" people can easily attain.

> The vague and tenuous hope that God is too kind to punish the ungodly has become a deadly opiate for the consciences of millions. It hushes their fears and allows them to practice all pleasant forms of iniquity while death draws every day

nearer and the command to repent goes unheeded. — A.W. Tozer

Sin Makes Us Gods

"God knows that your eyes will be opened as soon as you eat it, and you will be like God, knowing both good and evil." — Genesis 3:5

The third lie convinces us our disobedience is not rebellion against God, but that through our independence, we can become like Him. Satan says, *"as soon as you eat it, . . . you will be like God."* The spirit of this world flatters us. Rather than sin eternally separating us from God, he tells us sin will make us gods. He says we are in control and we alone determine what is right.

These lies teach us to put our hope in what we can accomplish in this life and to ignore eternal judgment. They tell us we can satisfy God's low standards and easy wrath by our own goodness. They are designed to make it impossible to fear the Lord and fully trust in Christ.

Deceived

We shouldn't be surprised when the spirit of this world successfully deceives outside the Church. That is to be expected. We should be concerned when the deception becomes dominant in the Church.

American sociologist, J.D. Hunter has dedicated much of his career to studying and writing about the state of Evangelicals in the United States. In his book, ***American Evangelicalism***, he explores shifts in the message of the modern church. He describes a "civilizing process" as follows: "The civilizing process entails de-emphasizing Evangelicalism's more offensive aspects: the notions of inherent evil, sinful conduct and lifestyles, the wrath of a righteous and jealous God, and eternal agony and death in hell."[1]

I don't know if Hunter realized that the "civilizing process" he identified in Evangelicalism agrees completely with the spirit of the world. This pervasive message directly opposes the work of the Holy Spirit. With this trend so widespread, should we wonder why many fall away and do not produce fruit?

It doesn't matter how clear the truth is. It doesn't matter how fervently it is received. The Gospel can't take hold in a heart that is in agreement with the spirit of this world on any point. The truth cannot change the heart and the eternal destiny of one who agrees with the spiritual powers of this world (Col. 2:8).

> *Sin whispers to the wicked, deep within their hearts. They have no fear of God at all. In their*

blind conceit, they cannot see how wicked they really are. — Psalm 36:1-2

We are attracted to and able to understand the message of the Kingdom when we fear the Lord.

Chapter 7

Fear of the Lord

The Gospel, the seed of truth, is the primary theme we find in the Bible. It tells us *what* God's plan is. Those convicted by the Holy Spirit, hearts with fertile soil, are the ones *who* benefit from God's plan. "What" and "who" are like two threads woven through God's Word.

The Bible illustrates the Spirit's conviction in many ways. One of the most common biblical descriptions of a prepared heart is one who fears the Lord. God expresses His extreme love and salvation to those who fear Him.

> *For his unfailing love toward those who fear him is as great as the height of the heavens above the earth.* — Psalm 103:11

What is the fear of the Lord? First, let's briefly address what it is not.

Natural Fear

The fear of the Lord is not like our day-to-day fears. We are selfish and naturally fear pain. The thought of going to Hell makes us want to avoid it. Fear of Hell is a fear like any other dread. People are afraid of war and sickness. Some may fear the future or different kinds of hardships. A healthy fear is an important part of self-preservation. It helps us avoid danger.

However, since this natural fear is selfish, so is the solution to that fear. We mistake the fear of the Lord with fear of judgment. Fear of God's judgment is self-centered, so it teaches us to look at ourselves for the solution. Self-help will not allow us to avoid God's wrath.

The magnificent cathedrals of Europe were built based on this selfish fear. During the Middle Ages, nearly any church you entered would have a painting of humans being brutally tortured in Purgatory, a temporary form of Hell invented by the Roman Catholic Church. A follower of Catholicism could shorten their time in Purgatory by donating to churches and paying for the services of priests. They thought they could literally buy their way out of Hell. These were useless attempts to alleviate the wrong kind of fear.

Today in the same way, many churches teach us we can buy our way into God's favor, and thus, out of Hell by our good works, giving, or devotion. Or that our efforts are a form of repayment for salvation. Attraction to these messages proves one thing; the fear the Lord is lacking.

Our own goodness will never appease God's wrath or match His holiness.

Supernatural Fear

The fear of the Lord is the work of the Spirit convicting of sin, God's righteousness, and the coming judgment. The Holy Spirit prepares our hearts to receive the Gospel in this way. He allows us to see our works are useless and cannot save us (Is. 64:6). The conviction in John 16, the fear of the Lord, and a prepared heart all describe those who will experience God's unfailing love and enter His Kingdom. They will seek and certainly find the truth.

Jesus did not hesitate to instill the fear of God's wrath in the hearts of His audiences. He was preparing the hearts of those who would soon see the Gospel unfold. He is preparing our hearts with the exact same words.

> *"Don't be afraid of those who want to kill your body; they cannot touch your soul. Fear only God, who can destroy both soul and body in hell."*
> — Matthew 10:28

A Just Fear

God is just and we are on the wrong side of His justice. The Holy Spirit confirms this fear. King David tells us:

He will judge the world with justice, and the nations with his truth. — Psalm 96:13b

As a child, I often got into trouble. My father consistently disciplined me. I feared his punishment simply because I wanted to avoid pain. There was one instance I will never forget. As my father hit me for blatantly disobeying him, I remember saying to myself, "I completely deserve this." For a brief moment, I realized my disobedience deserved punishment.

The fear of the Lord teaches us we deserve God's judgment. The Holy Spirit gives us a sense of justice when we think of His coming wrath. We aren't simply avoiding pain. When we consider eternity according to the Holy Spirit, we say to ourselves, "I have sinned against the holy Creator of all! I completely deserve His everlasting punishment."

As we read of examples in coming chapters, we'll see what the fear of the Lord causes in a heart. In its pure form, it is simple; this kind of fear is paralyzing terror at the thought of facing God based on our own "goodness." This fear convinces us that only Christ's free and undeserved mercy can satisfy God's justice.

Undeserved Mercy

The fear of the Lord teaches us that our escape requires far, far more than anything we could do or pay. As we grow to understand the eternal consequence of sin, we cling to the Gospel. We seek more knowledge of God's mercy, the seed of truth. When the Spirit convicts us, we are certain that His free and undeserved mercy is our only hope. The fear of the Lord teaches that Christ is our sole solution. It convinces us to cease trying to earn the impossible.

> *"He shows mercy from generation to generation to all who fear him."* — Luke 1:50

Do You Hate Sin?

Proverbs 8:13 says those who fear the Lord hate evil. It goes on to define evil with a list of sins. However, don't mistake pride for the fear of the Lord. Do you hate sin because it may be an embarrassment if it is exposed? That is the fear of man. Do you hate sin because it prevents you from attaining your ideal life? That is idolatry. The fear of the Lord teaches that your sins are an offense to God and invite His wrath!

A Complete Gospel?

You are not likely to hear much about Hell and God's judgment these days. Many churches neglect or obscure the elements of the conviction of the Spirit. Today, the most common version of Hell is merely an unfulfilled life.

Still, you will find some that teach God's judgment. If a message is aimed at stirring your natural fear of Hell and judgment rather than the fear of God, how will you know? What is the difference between preaching to natural fears rather than spiritual fear? Selfish fear always includes an escape that does not involve the free grace of God through Christ. The seed is corrupted. Sermons inspiring selfish fear convince you it's possible to help yourself out of Hell. But it is not possible. Self-help salvation proves the Spirit is not at work.

A complete Gospel message will include the consequence of sin *and* the sweet, unmerited grace of God available through Christ. The Spirit convinces us our condition is so dire that we hold tightly to His mercy and nothing else. As we'll discuss later, when this is understood, the fruit of our salvation starts to appear.

The Bible describes good soil in many other ways, all pointing to the effects of the work of the Spirit in preparing a heart.

Chapter 8

Humble Repentance

> Knowing God without knowing our own wretchedness makes for pride. Knowing our own wretchedness without knowing God makes for despair. Knowing Jesus Christ strikes the balance because he shows us both God and our own wretchedness. — Blaise Pascal

The parable of the Sower tells us Christian maturity requires "good soil." It is not very descriptive. It doesn't clarify the secret of what kind of heart embraces the seed. Similarly, the fear of the Lord is more descriptive, but it doesn't fully answer the question "who" has a prepared heart. However, the conviction of the Holy Spirit describes a prepared heart clearly (John 16:8).

What other biblical descriptions reveal the secret of who "good soil" represents? We'll look at some of the many ways the Bible illustrates a prepared heart. But first, we'll see what prepared soil is not.

Worldly Sorrow

> *But worldly sorrow, which lacks repentance, results in spiritual death.* — 2 Corinthians 7:10

Guilt and shame don't lead to true repentance. They are like selfish fear. Frustration with sin's earthly consequences results in worldly sorrow. It causes us to look for human solutions to help us deal with or overcome our sins without Christ. For this reason, the self-help industry will always succeed. Close behind its success will be "Christian" self-help. These industries prey on people's worldly sorrow, but offer no ultimate help.

Repentance is far more than making a promise to change our lives. It isn't simply a renewed effort to stop sinning and act like a Christian. Our nature won't let us keep these empty promises. Commitments to turn from sin without the fear of the Lord have no spiritual impact.

A Repentant Heart

> Repentance is not merely the start of the Christian life, it is the Christian life. — John Calvin

When the Spirit works in us, we are given the condition of a broken and contrite heart. This spirit of repentance continually reminds us that Christ alone can prevent our eternal separation from God. Holy fear teaches us sin is much more than an earthly inconvenience, so we cling to our Savior. A repentant heart is what allows us to abide in Christ (John 15:4).

All who fear the Lord will hate evil. — Proverbs 8:13a

As noted in the last chapter, the fear of the Lord teaches us to hate evil. The work of God's grace trains us to resist what we hate. The power of the Holy Spirit inspires this kind of repentance. This spiritual work transforms us more and more into the image of Christ (2 Cor. 3:18). Although, "*more and more*" tells us we shouldn't expect perfection in this lifetime.

Fertile soil represents a heart convicted to repentance by the Holy Spirit. This soil gladly embraces the seed of truth. It sprouts and thrives!

"The Kingdom of God is near! Repent of your sins and believe the Good News!" — Mark 1:15b

Humility

Humility is an excellent quality to have as we relate to those around us. It brings peace to our relationships. However, with few exceptions, humility in the Bible refers to an attitude we have toward God.

God's Word includes many examples of those who are blessed because they are humble toward their Creator. We mentioned the tax collector in chapter 1. Let's investigate what is happening below the surface.

> *"But the tax collector stood at a distance and dared not even lift his eyes to heaven as he prayed. Instead, he beat his chest in sorrow, saying, 'O God, be merciful to me, for I am a sinner.'"*
> — Luke 18:13

Notice his posture. The tax collector was at a distance and looking down. He *"beat his chest in sorrow."* His behavior tells us what was in his heart. He understood the weight of his sin and the distance it created between him and the Holy One.

The conviction of the Spirit caused him to confess his sin and cry out for mercy. Those who are humbled by the fear of the Lord will ask for and receive God's mercy. Again, Jesus tells us just who will enter His Kingdom.

> *"I tell you, this sinner, not the Pharisee, returned home justified before God. For those who exalt themselves will be humbled, and those who humble themselves will be exalted."* — Luke 18:14

God gives grace to the humble (James 4:6). Can there be a greater definition of humility than to clearly understand who we are before God? This is the fear of the Lord, the conviction of the Holy Spirit. A humble heart is fertile soil.

> Humility is the only soil in which the graces root.
> — Andrew Murray

We shouldn't expect God to grace us with humility toward others unless we have first been humbled toward Him.

The List Goes On

Here are a few examples of Holy Spirit-inspired fear of the Lord, or "good soil" found in the Word. Some are more descriptive than others, but each one mentions the qualities of those who will inherit God's Kingdom. Read the verses I've listed and see how they include ingredients of the Holy Spirit stirring hearts to the fear of the Lord.

- The first mention of fear in the Bible is when Adam and Eve were afraid to face God just after they brought sin into the world (Gen. 3:10).
- The fear of the Lord is *"godly sorrow"* (2 Cor. 7:11).
- It cultivates in us a *"broken and contrite spirit"* (Isa. 57:15).
- It affirms our spiritual poverty (Matt. 5:3).

- The fear of God proves we are sinners in need of the Great Physician (Mark 2:17).
- The *"godly"* fear the Lord, aren't afraid of God's justice, and bear fruit (Ps. 146:8, Prov. 12:12, 21:15).
- They have *"eyes to see and ears to hear"* the truth (Matt. 13:14-16).
- The spiritual can understand what the Spirit means (1 Cor. 2:14).
- Those who fear Him love the truth and recognize it (John 18:37).
- The Spirit prompts us to sincerely seek Him (Heb. 11:6).
- Jesus came to save those who know they are lost (Luke 19:10).
- The fear of the Lord is the beginning of wisdom, and wisdom is Christ (Ps. 111:10; 1 Cor. 1:24, 30; Isa. 33:6).
- All of those who are weary and burdened by sin's eternal consequence find rest in Christ (Matt. 11:28).
- Those who have faith do what is right and come into God's light rather than hate the light and refuse to go near it (John 3:18-21).
- In a list of basic elements of faith, Hebrews 6 mentions repentance, belief, and eternal judgment (Heb. 6:1-2).
- A hunger and thirst for God's righteousness proves we fear Him and are blessed (Matt. 5:6).

- When Paul spoke to Felix, the governor of Caesarea, and his wife, he *"reasoned with them about righteousness and self-control and the coming day of judgment"* (Acts 24:25).
- Prophecy and other miracles from the Spirit prompt hearers to *"be convicted of sin . . . their secret thoughts will be exposed, and they will fall to their knees and worship God, declaring, 'God is truly here among you'"* (1 Cor. 14:24-25).
- Jesus's miracle caused Peter to say, *"Oh, Lord, please leave me—I'm such a sinful man"* (Luke 5:8-9). He suddenly understood his wretchedness.
- *"We confess our sins"* because the Spirit has convinced us of our sinfulness; we are calling God a liar and do not have God's Spirit in us if we suppose our sin does not separate us from God (1 John 1:6-10).
- Two criminals hung on either side of Jesus when He was on the cross. The one who knew he deserved his punishment feared the Lord and entered the Kingdom of God. (Luke 23:40-43)

As our parable says, fertile soil gladly seeks and receives the seed. Let's look at some who describe their experience of receiving a prepared heart.

Chapter 9

God's Presence

What is it like to experience the fear of the Lord, to be convicted by the Holy Spirit? Who are those who experienced God's presence in tangible ways?

Through history we can see examples of people encountering God and experiencing the fear of the Lord. The Holy Spirit prepares people for the Gospel just like John 16:8 describes. As we study encounters with God, we learn what the work of the Holy Spirit provokes.

Biblical Conviction

The Bible tells us what occurs when God brings us near. Ezekiel was brought into God's presence (Ezek. 1:28). The book of Jonah tells us how the Spirit convicted the people of Nineveh (Jon. 3). Peter experienced the fear of the Lord when he saw Jesus do a miracle (Luke 5:8).

Each one had a close encounter with God's holiness. They saw the spiritual reality our natural eyes are blinded to. I encourage you to read these passages. Their responses are extremely similar. But for now, we'll review Isaiah's experience. Isaiah suddenly found himself in God's heavenly Temple. As he began to describe what he saw, he realized what it meant to be in the Almighty's righteous presence.

> *Then I said, "It's all over! I am doomed, for I am a sinful man. I have filthy lips, and I live among a people with filthy lips. Yet I have seen the King, the LORD of Heaven's Armies."* — Isaiah 6:5

Like Isaiah, we are doomed if we enter God's presence as we are. Our filth will never be allowed in the Temple of the holy Creator. However, God supplied a solution:

> *Then one of the seraphim flew to me with a burning coal he had taken from the altar with a pair of tongs. He touched my lips with it and said, "See, this coal has touched your lips. Now your guilt is removed, and your sins are forgiven."*
> — Isaiah 6:6-7

We see the soil—Isaiah's realization that he in his filth was doomed. He could not remain in God's presence. We see the seed at that time—God's generous way of purifying Isaiah so he could survive His terrifying holiness.

The fear of the Lord does not fade away once we hear and understand the Good News. John found himself in

Christ's presence after trusting and maturing in Him for many decades. He describes his experience.

> *"When I saw him, I fell at his feet as if I were dead." — Revelation 1:17a*

Jesus reminds John of His salvation just as the Holy Spirit does for us when we recall our sin's consequence.

> *But he laid his right hand on me and said, "Don't be afraid! I am the First and the Last."*
> *— Revelation 1:17b*

The Holy Spirit reminds us of our need for Christ and of His wonderful salvation. When we agree with the Spirit in this way, it deepens our love and faith in Him.

Flashes of God's presence were not only for those in biblical times. God's holy presence has appeared throughout Christian history. The Spirit's work causes reactions today that mirror the experiences of those mentioned in the Bible.

Historical Conviction

We have many firsthand accounts detailing the Great Awakening in the mid-eighteenth century. Evidence of the Holy Spirit's work swept through parts of northern Europe and North America. It had a major spiritual impact in these regions for generations. Jonathan Edwards and David Brainerd were evangelists in New England at the time and wrote about their meetings. These accounts describe large groups of people experiencing the conviction of the Holy Spirit. They were suddenly made aware of their sin, God's holiness, and the punishment to come. With hearts fully prepared, they quickly understood the truth, trusted in Christ, and rejoiced.

Jonathan Edwards

Edwards describes a meeting in December 1734 in Northampton, Massachusetts. "It was then a dreadful thing among us to lie out of Christ, in danger every part of dropping into hell; and what persons' minds were intent upon was, to escape for their lives, and to fly from the wrath to come."[2]

During Edwards's meetings, he noticed "an extraordinary sense of the awful majesty, greatness, and holiness of God, so as sometimes to overwhelm soul and body, a sense of the piercing, all-seeing eye of God so as to sometimes take away bodily strength; and an extraordinary view of the infinite terribleness of the wrath of God, together with a sense of the indescribable misery of sinners exposed to this wrath."[3]

His congregations were overwhelmed by the work of the Holy Spirit. Like the prophets mentioned above, many in these meetings fell on their faces as God drew near.

David Brainerd

David Brainerd was an evangelist to the Native Americans in New England. In 1744, he went from village to village preaching a simple Gospel message. He had preached the same messages before, but suddenly he noticed something was different. The Holy Spirit was working like he could never have imagined. His journal describes his surprising experience that summer. People, very young and old, "were made sensible of their misery without Christ." "They were almost universally praying and crying for mercy." He continues, "All were afraid of the anger of God, and of everlasting misery as the desert of sin."[4]

Brainerd tells of one girl who mocked him before his meeting but decided to come along anyway. She quickly became "so convinced of her sin and misery" that "she lay flat on the ground" calling out for God's mercy. She cried out in her native language over and over, "Have mercy on me, and help me to give you my heart!"[5]

Korea

Moves of God transformed society in Korea in the early 1900s. In a few short years, the church in Korea saw explosive growth. Meetings were similar to those of the Great Awakening in the United States over 150 years prior.

William Blair was a missionary in Korea at that time. He recounts God's work: "A spirit of heaviness and sorrow for sin came down upon the audience. Over on one side, someone began to weep, and in a moment the whole audience was weeping." He quotes a local pastor named Lee describing one parishioner who cried, "'Pastor, tell me, is there any hope for me, can I be forgiven?' and then threw himself to the floor and wept and wept, and almost screamed in agony"[6]

Can there be better descriptions of the Holy Spirit preparing hearts to receive the truth? In each instance, the Spirit suddenly filled hearts with the fear of the Lord.

Relief from Terror

In every case mentioned, the Holy Spirit didn't leave souls in anguish for long. They soon realized that Jesus was willing to freely lift their great burden of sin. They heard and understood the seed of truth, the message of the Kingdom. Brainerd describes the scenes of some who had gotten relief. "Those who had recently obtained relief were filled with comfort at this time. They appeared calm and composed, and seemed to rejoice in Christ Jesus; and some of them took their distressed friends by the hand, telling them of the goodness of Christ, and the comfort that is to be enjoyed in Him, and then invited them to come and give up their hearts to Him."[7]

They believed the truth about Jesus and received salvation, the eternal peace of God.

These evangelists are not alone. Movements in different time periods describe the same conviction. Diaries and biographies of those involved recount groups of people suddenly learning of their sin, God's holiness, and His coming wrath. They become convinced of their need for Christ. Relief and joy comes to those who trust Him.

Where we find written records of the Spirit persuading in this way, many evidences of Christian maturity begin to mark the local church.

Fully Spirit-Inspired

These leaders understood it had nothing to do with them. They didn't have a hand in producing it. It wasn't a matter of improving their church service or preaching style or of becoming more relevant. They continued to preach the truth in the same way they had before, focused on the complete Gospel message, but suddenly the Holy Spirit began to draw huge crowds and fill them with the fear of the Lord.

Edwards quotes David Brainerd from his journal on August 16, 1745:

> I never saw the work of God appear so independent of means as at this time. I taught the people, and spoke what, I suppose, had a proper tendency to promote convictions; but God's way of working in them appeared so entirely supernatural, and above my preaching style, that I couldn't believe he used me as an instrument, or what I said had any effect on carrying on his work; for it seemed, as I thought, to have no connection with, nor dependence on, my efforts in any way. . . . God seemed, as I understood, to work entirely without my methods. I seemed to do nothing, and indeed to have nothing to do, but to "stand still and see the salvation of God"; and found myself obliged and delighted to say, "Not unto us," not unto instruments and methods, "but to your name be glory." God appeared to work entirely alone, and I saw no room to attribute any part of this work to any created arm.[8]

These accounts describe true seed and rich soil meeting in many souls at once. They detail and agree with a sudden work of the Holy Spirit described in John 16. These are required for what some call "revival" to take place.

Distractions

When you hear people talk of Christian revival or renewal, yet you don't find true seed and fertile soil, be careful. Many messages deemed to be Christian disagree with the work of the Spirit in John 16. Intense emotion motivated by anything other than the terrifying conviction of the Holy Spirit and the joyous truth of the free grace of God through Christ means deception may be just around the corner. At best it will be a useless distraction.

What about today? Does the Holy Spirit work in the same way?

Chapter 10

Convinced

Personal Revival

Personal revival happens daily throughout the globe. God's presence is ever stirring hearts and opening eyes to see the light of truth. The Spirit is always convincing and convicting, more often in individual hearts than in large groups at once. God works in ways unique to each one. He has a personalized curriculum to teach us to grow in the fear of the Lord and in understanding.

Stunned

Some experience the work of the Holy Spirit in dramatic ways. Mary Poplin, a self-described former New Age, radical feminist professor, tells of her unexpected encounter with Jesus in a dream in the December 21, 2017, issue of *Christianity Today*: "When I got to Jesus and looked into his eyes, I grasped immediately that every cell in my body was filled with filth. Weeping, I fell at his feet. But when he reached over and touched my shoulders, I suddenly felt perfect peace!"

Later as she read the Bible and interacted with Christians, it became even more clear: "I had an experience like scales falling from my eyes. I suddenly realized that evil exists and, more importantly, it is in me."

> *And this veil can be removed only by believing in Christ. . . . But whenever someone turns to the Lord, the veil is taken away. For the Lord is the Spirit, and wherever the Spirit of the Lord is, there is freedom.* — 2 Corinthians 3:14b, 16-17

The Spirit gave Ms. Poplin a clear sense of her filth in God's sight. He showed her that Christ was the solution to the evil that filled her. He suddenly removed the veil that blinds us all. The Sower prepared her heart to receive the Gospel. These experiences seem more pronounced and dramatic for those who appear furthest from the truth.

Growing *to* Fear the Lord

> God sometimes does His work with gentle drizzle, not storms. — John Newton

In Daniel 4, King Nebuchadnezzar experienced God's conviction. He lost his mind and was driven away from society. For seven years, he was *"drenched with the dew of heaven"* (Dan. 4:33). When he returned to his senses, he feared the Lord. He proclaimed: *"Now I, Nebuchadnezzar, praise and glorify and honor the King of heaven. All his acts are just and true, and he is able to humble the proud"* (Dan. 4:37).

God's work in a heart often occurs gradually. It may take years for a soul to understand its need for Christ and finally trust in Him.

I collect testimonies. I love to hear stories of people's journey to Christ. One friend grew up in a country that is extremely hostile to the Gospel. He had a negative impression of Christianity. But he starts his testimony with, "I knew I was going to Hell."

The Spirit slowly began convicting him of his sin and its eternal consequence years before he learned of Jesus. Even still, his behavior grew more sinful and destructive when he moved to the United States. He lived in ever increasing despair.

A new friend invited him to church. The congregation began singing praises, and the words to a song stood out to him. They promised salvation through Christ, a salvation he had never heard of and didn't know was possible. After a little explanation, he trusted in Christ and matured quickly. He almost immediately joined an evangelistic group. He wanted to share his newfound freedom in Christ!

Growing *in* the Fear of the Lord

Before we trust in Christ, we grow *to* fear the Lord. We must see our need for Christ before we can hear and understand the message of the Kingdom. However, once we believe, we continue to grow *in* the fear of the Lord.

Most, like me, don't experience the work of the Spirit in such sensational ways. I experienced the conviction of the Holy Spirit to the point that I knew I needed saving. God gave me a tiny glimpse of my own arrogance. I believed the truth in my late teens. Although I gained knowledge of the Word, I didn't grow spiritually for many years. Finally, the realization that I didn't feel any appreciable love for God began to concern me. I confessed I didn't love God and came to understand I couldn't do anything about it. I cried out to Him for help.

God answered my prayer. Yet, rather than being suddenly overwhelmed with the fear of the Lord, the Holy Spirit slowly convinced me that my efforts to please Him were entirely useless. A steady marvel at God's grace developed in my heart. My view of His holiness grows off and on in small doses. I understand sin's eternal consequence, but at times it is more intense than others. As my awareness of these truths increases, so does my love for God.

I don't suppose anyone can perfectly fear the Lord in this life, but the Spirit will continually humble the hearts of believers. As humility grows in a heart, so does love and appreciation for the death and resurrection of Christ.

Honesty

We must be honest with God.

> *Jesus took the blind man by the hand and led him out of the village. Then, spitting on the man's eyes, he laid his hands on him and asked, "Can you see anything now?" The man looked around. "Yes," he said, "I see people, but I can't see them very clearly. They look like trees walking around." Then Jesus placed his hands on the man's eyes again, and his eyes were opened. His sight was completely restored, and he could see everything clearly.* — Mark 8:23-25

When we consider our trust in Christ, we may feel like the blind man. Our faith seems unclear or weak. We might have doubts about the Gospel and the fear of the Lord. When we suffer from spiritual nearsightedness, we should tell the Lord. Ask for more wisdom and conviction. Jesus will place His hands on our eyes. God is faithful to those who seek Him (Matt. 7:8-12).

> *If you need wisdom, ask our generous God, and he will give it to you. He will not rebuke you for asking.* — James 1:5

Horatius Bonar was honest. He was an evangelist in the 1800s. In his book, God's Way of Peace, he admits he was lying to God. He often confessed he was a sinner and needed God's grace. He knew the truth well, but he began to understand the truth alone wasn't enough. He realized his confessions were insincere. They came from an intellectual viewpoint, not from a sincere heart. Bonar confessed, "Lord, I do not feel like a sinner; I do not feel that I need mercy."[9]

From that moment on, something began to change. He experienced more and more of God's grace. The Spirit showed Bonar his need in a way that he couldn't acquire just by knowing, reciting, and even preaching the truth. God prepared his heart so he could fully embrace salvation. The Spirit blessed him with the fear of the Lord.

Call on Him

Has the Holy Spirit convicted and convinced you?

To find out, let's make things clear. There is a spiritual truth. It is a reality more tangible than anything we can view or touch on this earth. Few see or understand it. What is this truth? You are going to Hell. You are headed for eternal destruction, far from the presence of your holy Creator, because you are wretched in His sight. Jesus says the angels will throw you *"into the fiery furnace, where there will be weeping and gnashing of teeth"* (Matt. 13:42). Does this terrify you?

> *If we are afraid, it is for fear of punishment, and this shows that we have not fully experienced his perfect love.* — 1 John 4:18b

If the idea of eternal punishment scares you, or far worse, doesn't move you at all, there is hope! Let me tell you what to do. Beg for mercy. Cry out to the Holy Spirit. Ask Him to open your eyes to the Light of truth. The only hope you have is the grace of God expressed through Christ. Run to Him. Cling to Him!

> *For "Everyone who calls on the name of the Lord will be saved."* — Romans 10:13

Now, if you know you deserve God's wrath and the thought of eternal punishment prompts you to thank and praise Him for salvation through Christ, you are mature. The truth of the Gospel and the fear of the Lord are growing in your heart and have set you free. You have *"fully experienced his perfect love."*

You are ready for the question "how?" How do these ingredients make you spiritually mature?

Chapter 11

Deep Roots

Four seeds fell to the ground. The three that fell in bad soil had shallow, undeveloped roots, or no roots at all. We'll look at each of the conditions described in the parable and see how one seed grew and became fruitful while the others failed. First, let's lay the foundation of deep spiritual roots. Then it will be easier to see how some endure and why many can't.

How do roots grow? What is the secret to having deep, developed spiritual roots?

A Shift in Our Illustration

In the parable of the Sower, prepared soil is a heart that has been taught by the Spirit to fear the Lord. Deep roots represent a genuine believer. The Bible uses a wide variety of symbolism to describe those who will inherit the Kingdom of God. As we look at what gives us healthy roots, we'll make a shift in our illustration. These roots will still represent a believer, but "soil" will represent God's love, who is Christ. Mature roots grow deep into Christ, who has made His home in our hearts.

> *Let your roots grow down into him, and let your lives be built on him. Then your faith will grow strong in the truth you were taught, and you will overflow with thankfulness.* — Colossians 2:7

Growth Is Spiritual

The Holy Spirit leads us to the truth. The Holy Spirit convicts us. He opens our eyes to the spiritual reality of sin's eternal consequence. Now, we depend on the Spirit not only for birth but also for growth. A mortal human's relationship with the immortal, almighty God must, by definition, be supernatural. The Spirit empowers us to grow deep spiritual roots into Christ. What began by the Spirit must continue by the Spirit (Gal. 3:3).

> *I pray that from his glorious, unlimited resources he will empower you with inner strength through his Spirit. Then Christ will make his home in your hearts as you trust in him. Your roots will grow down into God's love and keep you strong.*
> — Ephesians 3:16-17

"Inner strength" comes from the *"glorious, unlimited resources"* of the Spirit. By His Spirit we develop confidence in and love for Christ. This faith and love fill us with the joy of the Lord.

Just How Do Deep Roots Develop?

Roots that keep us strong understand the dimensions of God's love. The passage in Ephesians 3 continues.

> *And may you have the power to understand, as all God's people should, how wide, how long, how high, and how deep his love is.* — Ephesians 3:18

The Lord leads His people *"into a full understanding and expression of the love of God that comes from Christ"* (2 Thess. 3:5a). How do we grow into that *"understanding and expression"?* Jesus tells us how.

An immoral woman understood, and so, expressed great love for Jesus at a dinner. She washed Jesus's feet with her tears and wiped them with her hair. She anointed His feet with a rare perfume and couldn't stop kissing them. She expressed the definition of genuine worship. Jesus's host, Simon, thought it was strange, but Jesus explained why she adored Him so much:

> *"A man loaned money to two people—500 pieces of silver to one and 50 pieces to the other. But neither of them could repay him, so he kindly forgave them both, canceling their debts. Who do you suppose loved him more after that?" Simon answered, "I suppose the one for whom he canceled*

> *the larger debt." "That's right," Jesus said.*
> — Luke 7:41b-43

A corrupted or incomplete human concept of what it is like to stand before our Creator gives us little appreciation for who He is and what Christ has mercifully accomplished. From a human standpoint, Jesus cancels only a small debt, if any. This kind of soil won't support spiritual growth. With mere intellect and emotion as our source, we shouldn't expect a great deal of genuine love for Christ.

> *For the person who keeps all of the laws except one is as guilty as a person who has broken all of God's laws.* — James 2:10

God's standard is much higher than ours. We can't imagine how one sin is enough to condemn us at judgment. Yet, each person's debt of sin, no matter what it may seem, far exceeds any payment imaginable. Therefore, the Spirit must convince us of our debt.

The great chasm between us in our willful rebellion and our holy God is immeasurable. To the same degree these vast extremes widen in our hearts, so does our understanding of the One who freely sacrificed His life to bridge that immense gap. As our view of the expanse between our sin and God's holiness increases, our love for Christ grows.

Jesus continues His illustration regarding the immoral woman in Luke 7, *"I tell you, her sins—and they are many—have been forgiven, so she has shown me much love."* As the reality of *"they are many"* becomes clear, so our appreciation for Christ builds. Our interest in self-esteem fades, and we learn to esteem Christ. We grow in our understanding of *"how wide, how long, how high, and how deep his love is"* as the Spirit shows us how wide, long, high, and deep the contrast is between our wretchedness and God's holiness.

The Joy of the Lord

The Spirit doesn't remind us of our wretchedness just once for salvation. He continues to work in us. Our eyes are opened more and more to the fear of the Lord. At the same time, we grow more convinced of God's gracious forgiveness through Christ, so our love for Him follows.

> *David also spoke of this when he described the happiness of those who are declared righteous without working for it: "Oh, what joy for those whose disobedience is forgiven, whose sins are put out of sight. Yes, what joy for those whose record the Lord has cleared of sin."* — Romans 4:6-8

King David was well known for his passionate love for God. He describes why those who understand the circumstances of their salvation express incredible joy. Although faith in Christ means we no longer fear judgment, we certainly remain aware of it. Joy and thanksgiving require context, so we continue to clearly recall our fate without Christ.

Where thoughts of sin and judgment are overwhelmed with the promise of God's mercy and grace through Christ, there is true worship. There is genuine joy and thanksgiving.

> The ultimate test of our spirituality is the measure of our amazement at the grace of God.
> — D. Martyn Lloyd-Jones

Spirit and Truth

> *"For God is Spirit, so those who worship him must worship in spirit and in truth."* — John 4:24

Many use worldly wisdom or emotion to try to stir up excitement about God. Humans will never experience genuine worship without the work of the Spirit. He must convince us of God's free and undeserved grace. He must remind us of the just punishment to come in the hereafter. These reminders enable us to worship in spirit and truth.

Seek out fellowship that values seed *and* soil. Sing songs that proclaim these truths, that highlight the great debt Jesus has canceled for us. Listen to sermons that don't neglect the free grace of God *and* the convictions of the Holy Spirit. In this context, you will most likely find mature spiritual fellowship and growth.

> *The church then had peace throughout Judea, Galilee, and Samaria, and it became stronger as the believers lived in the fear of the Lord. And with the encouragement of the Holy Spirit, it also grew in numbers.* — Acts 9:31

Chapter 12

Symptoms

Deep roots cultivated by the Spirit allow us to resist the world's distractions. They empower us to endure life's trials and live in obedience to God. There are four symptoms mentioned in our parable that indicate spiritual immaturity. Let's see how those who fear the Lord are different.

The first symptom—hearing but not understanding the Gospel—is the seed being snatched away. No roots develop in hard hearts, so the seed is left on the path for the birds. People hear the message of the Kingdom yet are not moved. They don't respond because they wholeheartedly agree with the spirit of this world.

Of course a prepared heart can hear and understand the truth under the Spirit's influence. That seems simple enough, so we'll move on to the next one.

> *"The seed on the rocky soil represents those who hear the message and immediately receive it with joy. But since they don't have deep roots, they don't last long. They fall away as soon as they*

> *have problems or are persecuted for believing God's word."* — Matthew 13:20-21

The second symptom—of those who hear and receive the seed with joy—is a failure to endure hardship or persecution. It's no wonder they don't understand and wither among the rocks. The Spirit has not convinced them of their distance from God and His justice in the hereafter. They value a good reputation in the present over eternal life. Seeds that sprout in rocky soil wilt, often in the face of the mildest persecution.

> I fear that some men would rather be damned than laughed at. — Charles Spurgeon

First, we'll see why suffering takes place. Then, we'll understand how a prepared heart handles suffering so much better than one that is unprepared.

Why Do Christians Suffer?

Humans have been using religious differences to hate and kill each other since Cain murdered Abel. Those who differentiate themselves through religion, no matter what religion, will suffer some form of persecution from others. Sinful nature compels humans to dislike or fear what is alien. Religious conflict, along with other kinds of strife, arises from this inborn fear and hatred of what is different.

Still, we who trust in Christ are offensive to others in a unique way. The light of Christ shines forth from our hearts. We emit the fragrance of Christ to those around us. It is *"a dreadful smell of death and doom"* to the world; our presence highlights sin in *"those who are perishing"* (2 Cor. 2:16). Those who are of the world are desperate to excuse sin and to hide it from the light of Christ (John 3:20).

Christians may endure trials simply because their values and customs are different from those around them. Yet, our true suffering is due to a spiritual difference. The Spirit's presence in us represents God's wrath to those who reject Christ's free gift.

Persecution, a Guarantee

Christians are guaranteed to face hardships for their faith. In 2 Timothy 3:12, the apostle Paul tells us that merely wanting to live a godly life will invite affliction. In John 15, Jesus promises the world will hate and persecute those who trust in Him. We shouldn't be surprised by such suffering, but rather rejoice that it proves we are partners with Christ (1 Pet. 4:12-13).

Stand Firm

That same Spirit that makes us offensive also provides endurance to the mature. Standing firm through suffering is a supernatural work of God.

> *It is God who enables us, along with you, to stand firm for Christ. He has commissioned us, and he has identified us as his own by placing the Holy Spirit in our hearts as the first installment that guarantees everything he has promised us.*
> — 2 Corinthians 1:21-22

Christians undergo varying degrees of persecution for trusting in Christ. It may be as little as a dirty look or mild ridicule when someone discovers we trust Jesus. Some may experience economic devastation, while others face rejection by family members. A few will be tortured and murdered for their faith.

How can we stand and even be joyful in the face of these trials? This verse tells us how: *"If you are insulted because you bear the name of Christ, you will be blessed, for the glorious Spirit of God rests upon you"* (1 Peter 4:14).

Since Christ suffered, we receive His joy when we endure problems caused by those who love darkness (1 Thess. 1:6). The Spirit who invites insults also rests on and comforts us in affliction.

Confidence

Those who hear and understand the Good News can have confidence when they face persecution for their faith. This assurance carries over to the general suffering all humans endure. Thankfully, the Spirit allows us to *"overflow with confident hope."*

> *I pray that God, the source of hope, will fill you completely with joy and peace because you trust in him. Then you will overflow with confident hope through the power of the Holy Spirit.*
> — Romans 15:13

Our Source of *"confident hope"* allows us to suffer in a unique context. Believers see suffering and trials from a broader perspective. Our view of life includes God's sovereignty. We know He has a purpose for everything.

> *And we know that God causes everything to work together for the good of those who love God and are called according to his purpose for them.*
> — Romans 8:28

Although we rarely understand why common suffering occurs, we rest in the promise that we will benefit from the difficulties we face.

Dear brothers and sisters, when troubles of any kind come your way, consider it an opportunity for great joy. For you know that when your faith is tested, your endurance has a chance to grow. So let it grow, for when your endurance is fully developed, you will be perfect and complete, needing nothing. — James 1:2-4

When we endure trials, we are promised maturity. We move away from our need for acceptance from the world. We are confident that hardships and forms of persecution are part of God's purpose. They allow us to grow more complete in our dependence on Christ.

It doesn't seem like it here on earth, yet we have already been blessed *with every spiritual blessing in the heavenly realms* (Eph. 1:3).

Chapter 13

Priorities

> *"The seed that fell among the thorns represents those who hear God's word, but all too quickly the message is crowded out by the worries of this life and the lure of wealth."* — Matthew 13:22a

The third symptom describes others who hear but don't understand the Gospel. They prefer success and wealth in this life. The Spirit has not given them a sense of eternity, so of course they prioritize worldly concerns over everlasting judgment.

Although they don't seem so concerned about persecution, shoots growing among the thorns are choked out by worldly distractions. These things *"dominate the thoughts of unbelievers"* (Luke 6:31-32).

"The worries of this life" manifest as obsessions with earthly fulfillment of various kinds. *"The lure of wealth"* keeps focus on financial security or excess. These are what unprepared hearts truly seek.

Mohammed immigrated to the United States from a Muslim country and became curious about Christianity. He started going to church and surrounded himself with Christian friends. For a time, he read the Bible daily. Within a year, he professed faith in Christ. He was convinced of the truth of the Gospel. Some of his friends in his home country ridiculed his decision and made fun of him. He was willing to endure persecution, but after a few years he became disillusioned. He told me his finances and opportunities hadn't improved as he had expected. He asked, "What's the use of being a Christian if God won't answer my prayers?" He revealed what his true concerns were.

Mohammed heard and received the truth. But since he was convinced only of an earthly need for Christ, he never understood. His faith was in a corrupted salvation, one that promised to fulfill temporal concerns. He could not mature and produce fruit.

Christ Overcomes

Now let's see why a heart prepared by the Holy Spirit is not distracted by the world's priorities.

> *For every child of God defeats this evil world, and we achieve this victory through our faith. And*

> *who can win this battle against the world? Only those who believe that Jesus is the Son of God.*
> — 1 John 5:4-5

Faith in Christ brings a supernatural change in priorities. It guarantees success against the world's way of thinking. In some ways, the transformation may be immediate; in others ways, more gradual. Blessed with the *"mind of Christ"* (1 Cor. 2:16), His priorities become ours. He gives us the strength we need to resist the idols of success and riches.

Eternal Perspective

Shallow roots that wither and die are pitiful. They have little or no eternal hope.

> *And if our hope in Christ is only for this life, we are more to be pitied than anyone in the world.*
> — 1 Corinthians 15:19

The work of the Spirit gives believers a growing eternal perspective. We have eternity in our hearts. Our view of time is not available to the natural mind. The Spirit has revealed to us the *coming* judgment, so our hearts are opened to the everlasting.

A Christian is able to put the cares of this life in their proper context. Carnal hope for earthly success transitions into a confident hope to remain in God's presence forever.

> *"Those who love their life in this world will lose it. Those who care nothing for their life in this world will keep it for eternity."* — John 12:25

A sense of the everlasting changes our perspective. The Spirit makes it easier to deal with life's temptations and unpredictable events as we grow to possess a *"confident hope of what God has reserved for you in heaven"* (Col. 1:5).

> *Since you have been raised to new life with Christ, set your sights on the realities of heaven, where Christ sits in the place of honor at God's right hand. Think about the things of heaven, not the things of earth.* — Colossians 3:1-2

No one knows what will happen tomorrow, so don't worry about the future in this life (Matt. 6:34). However, we can rejoice and endure because the Holy Spirit has given us a glimpse of eternity.

Better Things Await

Can you imagine being thrown into jail and losing all your possessions because you won't renounce Christ? This and much worse has been happening throughout church history. The apostle Paul addresses a group who lost everything because of their faith: "*You suffered along with those who were thrown into jail, and when all you owned was taken from you, you accepted it with joy. You knew there were better things waiting for you that will last forever*" (Heb. 10:34).

How were they supposed to have joy when everything was taken from them? They weren't obsessed with worldly definitions of success and riches. Earthly possessions held little value because their hope was in what will last forever. What value does momentary security compare to a guarantee of eternal peace in the presence of God?

> *Because of his grace he made us right in his sight and gave us confidence that we will inherit eternal life.* — Titus 3:7

The Gospel at work in a prepared heart not only crowds out the *worries of this life* and the *lure of wealth*. To possess deep roots in Christ means the Spirit changes our view of life and death.

> *If we live, it's to honor the Lord. And if we die, it's to honor the Lord. So whether we live or die, we belong to the Lord.* — Romans 14:8

Eyes opened to immortality, death begins to lose its earthly meaning. What is important is that we belong to Christ. So what on earth should we fear? Certainly not the trials of life and persecution from *"those who are perishing"* (2 Cor. 2:16).

> *So we can say with confidence, "The Lord is my helper, so I will have no fear. What can mere people do to me?"* — Hebrews 13:6

Pray

Jesus knows we struggle with the world's priorities. He tells us to cry out to Him for rescue from being obsessed with earthly concerns and attraction to wealth. Jesus teaches us to pray; *"And don't let us yield to temptation, but rescue us from the evil one"* (Matt. 6:13).

We must rely on Jesus because our nature alone cannot resist the spirit of this world. The evil one's influence surrounds us day and night. What hope does our weak nature have against continual temptation to conform?

Thankfully, the Spirit of God alive within us is more powerful and always at work keeping us from being dominated by the ways of the world.

The Spirit who lives in you is greater than the spirit who lives in the world. — 1 John 4:4b

Chapter 14

Lasting Fruit

The fourth symptom in the parable of the Sower is a lack of genuine spiritual fruit. Only the seed that fell in rich soil produced a harvest.

> *"The seed that fell on good soil represents those who truly hear and understand God's word and produce a harvest of thirty, sixty, or even a hundred times as much as had been planted!"*
> — Matthew 13:23

For those convinced and convicted by the Spirit, fruit is genuine and eternal. It wells up inside a believer. It is written on our hearts (Ps. 40:8). All who can *"truly hear and understand God's word"* spiritually thrive and mature.

Genuine fruit is never produced in an attempt to impress God or pay for salvation. Christ alone is capable of saving us. Spiritual fruit is a product of being led by the Spirit, a promise for all who trust in Jesus (Rom. 8:14).

We abide in Christ because the Spirit continually reminds us of our plight and the salvation He has supplied. More and more aware of what our destiny would be without Christ, we remain evermore reliant on the Vine. Those with prepared hearts can't help but produce fruit since Jesus is their source.

> *"Yes, I am the vine; you are the branches. Those who remain in me, and I in them, will produce much fruit. For apart from me you can do nothing."* — John 15:5

We've seen fruit in a general context: good fruit, spiritual fruit, lasting fruit, abundant fruit. These qualities indicate the fruit must be from the Vine, but they don't describe what that fruit is like. However, the New Testament mentions four specific kinds of fruit. Let's explore what the Spirit produces in the life of a believer.

Righteous Character

No matter how good humans can seem, their fallen nature can't produce even the smallest thought or act of *pure* righteousness. If that were possible, there would be no need for a Savior at all. Yet, a wonderful benefit of faith in Jesus is being transformed into His likeness (Rom. 12:2). The Spirit develops the desires of Christ in us over our lifetime and clears away our preference for sin.

> *May you always be filled with the fruit of your salvation—the righteous character produced in your life by Jesus Christ—for this will bring much glory and praise to God.* — Philippians 1:11

God is working His desires into our hearts so we can please Him (Phil. 2:13). The power of the Gospel changes our lives (Col. 1:6). Biblical values are impossible to live out genuinely if the Spirit is not within us. But filled with His power, they grow to become *our* hearts' desires. In his letter to the Galatians, Paul lists some of the character traits that come from the Spirit.

> *But the Holy Spirit produces this kind of fruit in our lives: love, joy, peace, patience, kindness, goodness, faithfulness, gentleness, and self-control. There is no law against these things!*
> — Galatians 5:22-23

We won't reach perfection in this life, but we can be certain of these promises. The Spirit will change us, although He may not do it as quickly and completely as we would like.

Praise to God

A symptom of growing deep roots into Christ is praise. As the Spirit reminds us of the circumstances of our salvation, we bear the fruit of praise to God. Worship is a normal part of Christian life. Thanksgiving springs from hearts overwhelmed by the thought of God's grace.

> *Through him then let us continually offer up a sacrifice of praise to God, that is, the fruit of lips that acknowledge his name.*
> — Hebrews 13:15 (ESV)

Praise may occur during a church service where we are reminded of God's mercy. The Spirit may prompt us to recall the extremes of our salvation at any time, maybe many times through our day. From a brief thought of God's undeserved mercy to overwhelming periods of thanksgiving—all are acceptable day or night.

Good Deeds

> *But the wisdom from above is first of all pure. It is also peace loving, gentle at all times, and willing to yield to others. It is full of mercy and the fruit of good deeds.* — James 3:17a

The wisdom we receive inspires good deeds done in sincerity. Human nature demands payment or glory in exchange for good works. Deep down we all want to be seen or rewarded for "goodness." However, the fruit of the Spirit is different. To bear this fruit may or may not win us praise, but in bearing it, we act selflessly, expecting nothing in return (Acts 20:35).

Harvest of Souls

Of course, those who experience such a great salvation want others to know the truth. Believers are led by the Spirit to share their faith and lives with those around them. Spiritual fruit represents souls who learn to trust in Christ.

I like the illustration given in 1 Corinthians 3:7: *"It's not important who does the planting, or who does the watering. What's important is that God makes the seed grow."*

The Holy Spirit convicts and convinces our neighbors of the truth. Our role—planting and watering—is simple obedience. Christians will notice God places *"those who know they are sinners"* around us (remember, it is these whom Jesus came to save). We emit the fragrance of Christ, so God will arrange for us to encounter those seeking the truth (2 Cor. 2:15). How do we plant and water?

Planting

The parable tells us each seed represents a person who hears the Gospel. Some reject the Good News; others receive it yet don't understand. The point is, all were told the message of the Kingdom. We could say "planting" is telling people the Gospel, or at least inviting them to a place where they can hear it clearly.

We make sure they hear a Gospel message that agrees with the Spirit. The complete Gospel message includes the truth of willful human wretchedness, God's righteousness, and the coming judgment (John 16:8). It assures that Christ alone makes us pure and holy in God's sight by His free and undeserved grace (John 14:6; Rom. 11:6).

Paul addressed the high council in Athens. He finished his appeal at the end of Acts 17 telling them about the coming judgment. Many laughed at what he said. Yet, those who wanted to hear more joined him and trusted in Christ. Paul's preaching followed the conviction of the Holy Spirit. He was able to find those who feared God and invest in them rather than the scoffers.

True seekers are not scared off by the mention of sin and judgment. They are willing to endure God's light (John 3:21). Deep down, they are searching for a solution to their rebellion against God, although they may not realize it right away. When unbelievers increasingly pursue the fellowship of Christians and don't flee from the complete Gospel message, it is just a matter of time before they understand.

A Hindu and a Muslim were discussing the Bible study topic, our need for Christ. The Hindu concluded, "It doesn't matter what you believe, just pick something and stick with it. Then you'll be fine." The Muslim replied, "I have to face God one day. I can't just pick anything. I have to know the truth!" Later that evening he asked us to pray that God would show him the truth. The Hindu soon stopped engaging with believers, but the Muslim continues to seek out Christian fellowship so he can discuss the Gospel.

Farming Requires Patience

Since "*God makes the seed grow*," there is no urgency for a decision. Souls persuaded by the Spirit don't need to be pressured or rushed to faith. We are confident God will finish the work He started (Phil. 1:6).

> "By the grace of God we will never pluck unripe fruit. We will never press people to decision, because we'll lead them to damnation and not salvation." — Jonathan Edwards

Seeds planted in good soil will certainly sprout, shoots will appear above the surface. When those growing to fear the Lord do finally express their faith, they will mature quickly.

Watering

To continue with our illustration, watering is living out the fruit of the Spirit with unbelievers. Sincere seekers are refreshed and attracted by this fruit displayed through believers.

We may walk along with those who smell the fragrance of Christ in us for decades and see harvest when they finally understand the Gospel. It's possible that our role in someone's journey toward Christ will be as small as an act of hospitality at the right moment or a single conversation. We may never learn, in this life, of the way the Spirit did His work through us in helping someone come to an understanding of the truth. We look forward to learning what God has done through us when we reach His presence in eternity.

God will give us contentment, patience, and the words to say as we live life alongside those seeking the truth.

Invite those who seem to be attracted to Christ to spend time with you and enjoy fellowship with other Christians. In so doing, you and your fellow believers will drench seeds with water from the Spirit.

God Makes the Seed Grow

> *"Humans can reproduce only human life, but the Holy Spirit gives birth to spiritual life."* — John 3:6

Humans may be able to persuade each other of the logic of the Gospel. They may prove Christianity is superior as a religion. Nevertheless, human wisdom can never lead to *"spiritual life."*

Evangelism completely depends on the Holy Spirit. He alone can convince and convict (John 6:63).

I know a man from Central Asia who despised the Christian religion. He described layers of hate for all things Christian. He spent his life wanting to kill Christians. He heard John 3:16 one time, and in a few seconds his deep hatred was gone and he believed the Gospel. He immediately dedicated his life to telling others about Christ in an environment where he would experience severe persecution. Can we credit the one who read the verse for this sudden and extraordinary transformation? Of course not.

I know others who were attracted to Christian fellowship and the Gospel message for years. They heard the Good News of Christ many, many times before they finally trusted Him. They didn't realize the Spirit was drawing them until the moment they understood. In every case, it is God's power that saves. He works uniquely in each person.

United for the Gospel

One thing is sure. Those who fear the Lord will work together to spread the Good News of Christ and will see spiritual fruit. All are gifted differently. Each has a unique role, but our purpose is the same: to spread the message of the Kingdom and to bear eternal fruit.

> *. . . you are standing together with one spirit and one purpose, fighting together for the faith, which is the Good News.* — Philippians 1:27b

Chapter 15

Falling Away

We've seen how the mature endure and produce fruit. How about those who don't? Why do so many fall away and lack genuine fruit?

As noted in chapter 4, the truth of the Gospel alone cannot save. The seed by itself will never lead to maturity. However, it is possible to construct large movements based on principles found in the New Testament. The message of the Kingdom on its own can stimulate intellect and emotion without the work of the Spirit. Such movements and the congregations influenced by them are established in the poor soil described in our parable.

Humans have built massive religions based on far inferior books and values than those underlying Christianity. Wouldn't a movement based on Christian principles be even better?

The seeds that fell among the rocks and in the thorns represent this pervasive religion. They gladly receive the message of the Kingdom, but without conviction, they never understand it. We see this false "faith" in Judas, who followed Jesus but never believed. This is the same faith the apostle Paul's fellow worker and evangelist Demas had. He preached the Gospel beside Paul, yet he was lured away (2 Tim. 4:10). This is the religion of the *"many"* we read about in Matthew 7:22 who will be surprised on Judgment Day. The New Testament describes this version of a Christianity that lacks power (2 Tim. 3:5), one that caters to what people want to hear rather than the Gospel (2 Tim. 4:3).

Thankfully, the parable of the Sower tells us what to expect where fertile soil is missing. These belief systems avoid two things: the free and undeserved grace of God expressed through Christ and the everlasting consequence of sin in light of God's holiness. They ignore or corrupt at least one, but more likely both.

These messages attract and feed on those with unprepared hearts, hearts that cannot mature. They confuse true seekers who never learn how to be pure in God's sight. They disappoint believers because they don't inspire worship of God, but ultimately of self. We should never expect maturity where the message of the Holy Spirit is lost.

First, we'll describe what congregations of rocky soil look like. Then, in the next chapter we'll discuss those who languish among the thorns.

Rocky Congregations

How would you attract those who can't handle persecution?

Shoots that grow in rocky soil eventually wither when persecution occurs. As the difference grows between society's values and Christian values, remaining in a faith tradition becomes more difficult to endure. So, in order to avoid being associated with unpopular beliefs, some simply leave their traditions.

Others, however, still clinging to Christian traditions, seek a message bent to conform to social norms. They settle on a new set of values that won't offend their peers, and thereby prevent persecution. These congregations remove the authority of the Word, then pick and choose biblical principles that appeal most to the worldly values that surround them.

Jesus was a good moral example, so they base a religion on elements of His ministry that seem acceptable to unbelievers. They follow these ideals to satisfy their lust for society's approval. They fulfill their selfish needs for esteem by touting their moral superiority. They don't realize that by creating a "modern" set of values, they fall for the oldest trick in the book, the deceptions covered in chapter 6.

Sin to those in rocky soil isn't willful rebellion against our holy Creator. It is an inconvenience that certainly won't lead to judgment. It becomes a form of brokenness that turns them into victims of various forms of oppression. Remember, they can't handle persecution. Rather than take responsibility for their own sins before God and man, they blame perceived oppressors for their ills.

They may be willing to suffer for a wide variety of religious ideals. Yet, they will not endure hardship for the sake of the complete Gospel message. Their earthly wisdom will not allow it.

They prove they never belonged when they reject the Church and its teaching (1 John 2:19).

> If you believe in the Bible what you like, and leave out what you don't like, it's not the Bible you believe but yourself. — Augustine of Hippo

Consequence

Like all who will not inherit eternal life, those who fall away trust in their own goodness instead of Christ's. They make a god in their own image and a religion that agrees with the spirit of this world. They turn away from the God of the Bible and follow a way that twists the truth (Gal. 1:6-7).

In doing so they prove they never understood their separation from God. They will not experience His grace. Instead, His anger will fall on them (Eph. 5:3-6). They become the weeds that grow among the wheat. They are described in Matthew chapter 13 following the explanation of the Parable of the Sower. In the end, they are sorted out and burned.

Will the fate of the fruitless be any different?

Chapter 16

Cut Off

> *"The seed that fell among the thorns represents those who hear God's word, but all too quickly the message is crowded out by the worries of this life and the lure of wealth, so no fruit is produced."*
> — Matthew 13:22

The last description of those whose hearts are unprepared is a lack of genuine fruit. True seed is sown in each heart; however, in those lacking fertile soil, the result is no lasting fruit.

We learned in chapter 5 that those with unprepared hearts *"aren't spiritual"* and *"can't receive these truths"* (1 Cor. 2:14). So, how could one produce spiritual fruit without God's Spirit? It's impossible. True fruit does not develop by mere human will (Phil. 3:3). Every aspect is Spirit-driven.

Plants in thorny soil don't understand the severity of their sin and assume their goodness can satisfy God's wrath. Their faith is not in Christ, but in themselves.

Human pride motivates everyone to project some form of goodness. Although this goodness may look a lot like Christian fruit, it is not the same. Many bear a type of fruit they suppose will impress God and others in their church. They are like those Jesus rejects on Judgment Day who we discussed in chapter 3. Even though their works are performed in Jesus's name, their fruit is not from the Spirit.

> Virtues without faith are whitewashed sins.
> — Charles Spurgeon

"Fruit" produced in a Christian context, yet cultivated in an attempt to pay for God's favor is not genuine. Galatians 5:4 tells us if you *"are trying to make yourselves right with God by keeping the law,"* you have been *"cut off from Christ"* and *"have fallen away from God's grace."*

Virtues attained or works displayed in order to appease God's wrath or earn salvation take Christ's place in our hearts. 1 John 5:21 tells us that is idolatry!

Thorny Congregations

Those who are obsessed with life's worries and lured away by wealth share the worlds concerns but prefer to live out and uphold Christian values and traditions. How would you appeal to those *"cut off from Christ"* who believe they can earn their salvation?

These groups focus on earthly solutions to life's problems and avoid the issue of eternity. Salvation becomes a way to attain happiness and fulfillment in this life or as a method to treat temporal anxieties. They seek solutions to the "*worries of this life*" largely or completely without Christ. Congregants crave biblical formulas that promise financial security or excess to entertain the "*lure of wealth.*"

Since their efforts won't generate the material and emotional rewards they expect, they live in disappointment.

Their pastors may call out specific sins that bring shame before men, but not the wretched state that eternally condemns before the living God. In all of this, they present salvation as a mere cure for sin's inconveniences and Jesus as a good luck charm that will make earthly dreams come true.

Shoots who are choked out by thorns affirm the Bible is God's Word. They may hold strongly to Christian habits and traditions. They are willing to endure degrees of persecution for their religion. But their true interest is what God can do for them in this life.

> *Jesus replied, "I tell you the truth, you want to be with me because I fed you, not because you understood the miraculous signs."* — John 6:26

Messages aimed at seeds fallen in thorns will only sustain people's attendance, maybe their participation (2 Tim. 4:3). However, pandering to bad soil will prove tragically useless in eternity.

Don't be fooled by movements that masquerade as Christianity yet don't depend on the power of the Holy Spirit to offer truth and conviction.

Faith?

As discussed in chapter 3, Jesus initiates and perfects our faith (Heb. 12:2). He is our sole source (1 Tim. 1:14). Some will speak of a different kind of faith. One that comes from themselves. This is not faith in Christ for salvation from eternal judgment. Faith for them is convincing themselves that God will prevent their worldly worries from occurring and enrich them with earthly blessings.

They may experience the miraculous. These miracles may give their "faith" legitimacy. Nevertheless, since their experiences aren't coupled with the conviction of the Holy Spirit as they should be (1 Cor. 14:24, Luke 5:8-9), they won't promote true spiritual growth.

Detached

None of the seeds that fell in bad soil produced fruit. Jesus tells us their fate. In Matthew 3:10 and 7:19, He says those without good fruit are *"chopped down and thrown into the fire."* They are like branches detached from the vine and, therefore, unable to produce genuine fruit.

> *"Anyone who does not remain in me is thrown away like a useless branch and withers. Such branches are gathered into a pile to be burned."*
> — John 15:6

Those who don't remain in Christ will initially receive the Gospel with joy, but with unprepared hearts they lack understanding. The message of the Kingdom is crowded out. They inherit the terrifying consequence of being spiritually fruitless.

If you are concerned that you aren't seeing genuine, spiritual fruit in your life, reread the first few chapters of this book. Seek the work of the Holy Spirit as described by Jesus in John 16. Pray that your eyes will be opened to the magnitude of your sin in God's sight! Only in that way will you remain in Christ.

Chapter 17

Conclusions

In Mark 4, Jesus starts His private explanation of the parable of the Sower by exhorting the disciples: *"If you can't understand the meaning of this parable, how will you understand all the other parables?"* (Mark 4:13).

The truths exposed in this parable shine light on all of Jesus's illustrations. They exhort us to seek out two critical biblical themes: what the truth of the Gospel is, and who those are who benefit from it. As you read the Word of God, ask the Spirit to open your eyes to these themes. When understood, they lead to eternal rest in the presence of God. They lead to supernatural peace and the fruit of the Spirit in this life.

Prayer

Perhaps the most important lesson one who trusts in Christ can take away from the parable of the Sower is how to pray.

We pray for the work of the Spirit in those around us and the world. Whether they already have faith in Jesus or not, our prayer remains the same. We are confident that, as the Spirit helps our neighbor truly hear and understand the Gospel full of His conviction, they will certainly grow in, or into, belief and thrive. The Spirit will bring faith and maturity through increasing conviction. They will grow to stand in Christ confidently on their own (2 Cor. 1:24).

We pray for our leaders, especially Christian leaders, in the same way. They face all forms of difficulties. However, the work of the Spirit is the ultimate solution. A better understanding of their distance from God without Christ will send them running to Him all the more. There can be no greater benefit.

As we consider our own faith, we cry out for more of God's grace. We ask specifically for more of the fear of the Lord and a clearer understanding of His truth. As God answers these prayers, we mature. Connected to the Vine, we produce spiritual fruit.

Discernment

To understand these themes by the Spirit not only leads to Christian maturity; it also helps us discern where the Gospel is honestly represented. As noted countless times in this book:

- The seed represents the sweet, undeserved grace of God through Christ to save eternally all who believe.
- The soil represents the convicting power of the Holy Spirit to convince souls of their unrighteousness, God's holiness, and the judgment to come. Fertile soil means a soul understands his or her desperate need for Christ.

In any Christian fellowship where either or both messages are consistently being avoided or ignored—or worse, corrupted—don't expect genuine spiritual growth. Don't expect to find worship in Spirit and in truth.

On the other hand, where we are commonly taught and reminded of the free grace of God and the elements of the fear of the Lord, we should find the fruit of the Spirit at work. This kind of fellowship will build us up and be an effective witness.

> *This same Good News that came to you is going out all over the world. It is bearing fruit everywhere by changing lives, just as it changed your lives from the day you first heard and understood the truth about God's wonderful grace.*
> — Colossians 1:6

Suffer Well

This fallen world we live in produces far more adversities in life than those mentioned in the parable of the Sower. We will experience tragedies, hardships, and trials of all kinds. Peter tells us the purpose of our Spirit-driven endurance:

> *So be truly glad. There is wonderful joy ahead, even though you must endure many trials for a little while. These trials will show that your faith is genuine. It is being tested as fire tests and purifies gold—though your faith is far more precious than mere gold. So when your faith remains strong through many trials, it will bring you much praise and glory and honor on the day when Jesus Christ is revealed to the whole world.* — 1 Peter 1:6-7

Our life here on earth is a mere *"morning fog—it's here a little while, then it's gone"* (James 4:14). Persistence through suffering in this brief life refines and proves our hold on Christ. This purified faith produces a kind of eternal treasure valued in heaven.

As we've seen in previous chapters, the New Testament writers tell us to look to our glorious future as we endure hardships. Convinced by the Spirit of the *coming* judgment, our eyes are opened to the eternal in a way we couldn't see before we trusted Christ. This is how we are able to look continually beyond this life as we suffer. Peter goes on: *"Put all your hope in the gracious salvation that will come to you when Jesus Christ is revealed to the world"* (1 Peter 1:13b).

Wisdom's End

God blessed King Solomon with supernatural wisdom. In the book of Ecclesiastes, Solomon begins by letting us know everything in life is *"completely meaningless"* (Eccles. 1:2). Thankfully, his conclusion is more encouraging.

> *That's the whole story. Here now is my final conclusion: Fear God and obey his commands, for this is everyone's duty.* — Ecclesiastes 12:13

I pray we can take his advice. Fear God and believe the message of the Kingdom!

Note from the author:

Thank you for reading this book! I wrote it for you. If you found it helpful, please recommend it to your friends and family.

Consider taking a few minutes to write a review online. It may encourage others to read it. You can access this information at the following website:

www.theparableoftheSower.com

or follow the book on Instagram:

www.instagram.com/theparableofthesower

May you grow fully into the truth and the fear of the Lord,

M.S. Muse
theparableoftheSower@yahoo.com

Endnotes

1 J. D. Hunter, *American Evangelicalism*, 87.
2 Jonathan Edwards, *The Works of President Edwards*, 114.
3 Ibid., 303.
4 Jonathan Edwards, *The Life and Diary of David Brainerd*, 296.
5 Ibid., 284.
6 William Blair, *Korean Pentecost*, 46-47.
7 Jonathan Edwards, *The Life and Diary of David Brainerd*, 297.
8 Ibid., 224
9 Horatius Bonar, *God's Way of Peace*, 173

Printed in Great Britain
by Amazon